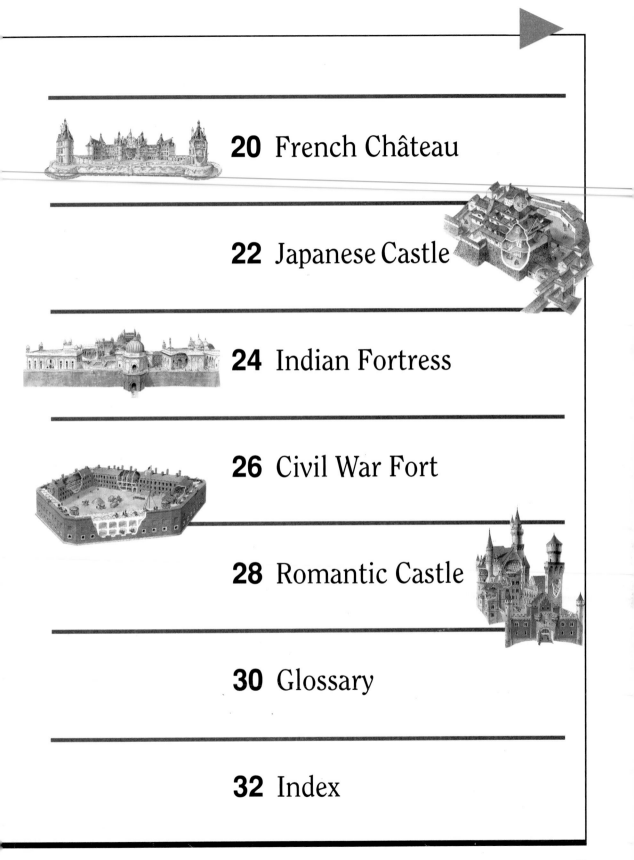

Bronze Age Citadel

4 Royal tombs were built into the hillside. They consisted of long passages with rooms cut out of the rock at the ends.

5 The palace was finely decorated. The walls were covered with wall paintings called frescoes. The floors were covered in plaster and then decorated.

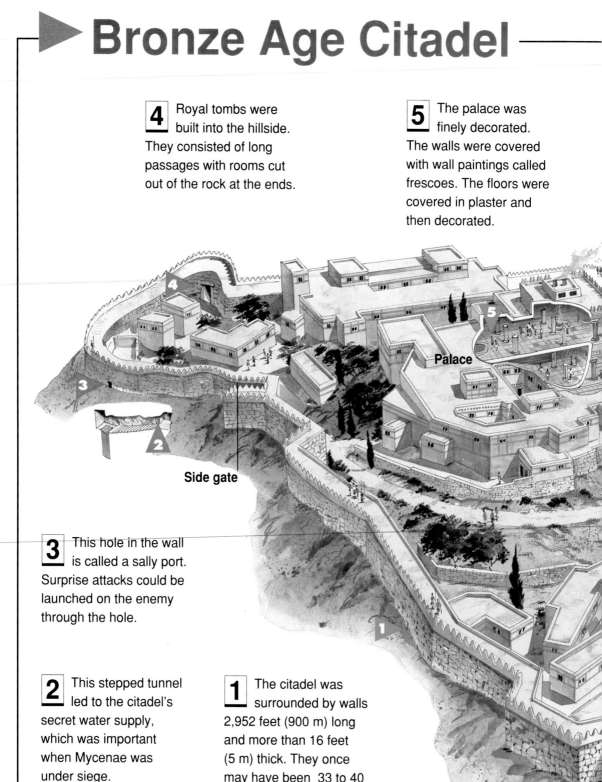

Palace

Side gate

3 This hole in the wall is called a sally port. Surprise attacks could be launched on the enemy through the hole.

2 This stepped tunnel led to the citadel's secret water supply, which was important when Mycenae was under siege.

1 The citadel was surrounded by walls 2,952 feet (900 m) long and more than 16 feet (5 m) thick. They once may have been 33 to 40 feet (10 to 12 m) high and were built of stone.

Foreword

From earliest times, people have gathered into fortified camps for defense against an enemy. If possible, these camps were built on hilltops and called strongholds or forts. Our word *fort* comes from the Latin word *fortis*, meaning "strong."

As time went on, these forts became more sophisticated. Stronger walls were built. Larger and improved living quarters were constructed. These more advanced fortresses were called castles. The word *castle* means a large fortified building or group of buildings. Some castles were magnificent homes.

Life in a castle was constant preparation for war. Attackers used powerful catapults to hurl rocks and other missiles at castle walls. Castle archers fired crossbows at the enemy through the castle's slitlike windows.

With the development of gunpowder, castles could not protect their inhabitants as well. Cannon fire could destroy all but the strongest walls. The usefulness of castles had come to an end.

Many of the ancient castles and forts we visit today seem empty and silent. But in their day, they were noisy, bustling, colorful places.

Contents

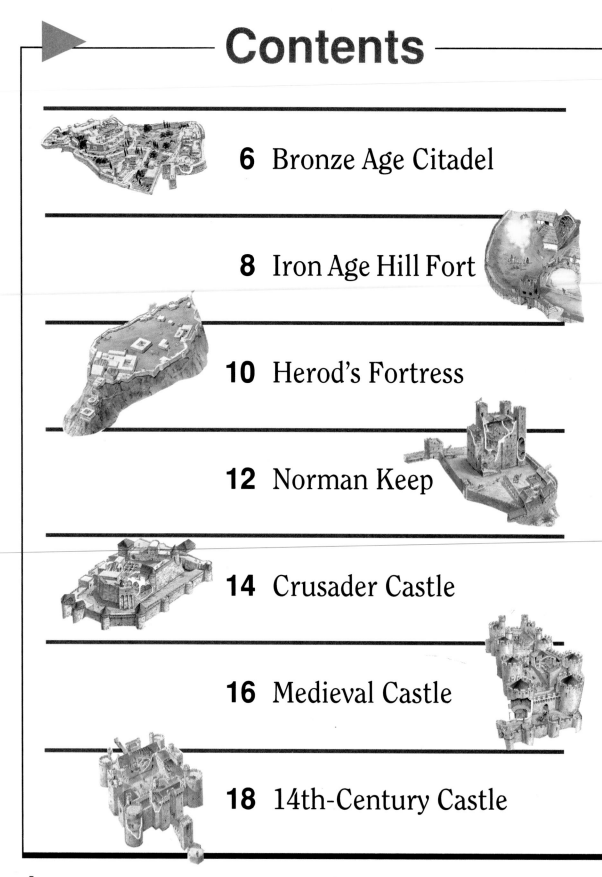

POINTERS

FORTS AND CASTLES

Written by Miriam Moss
Illustrated by Chris Forsey

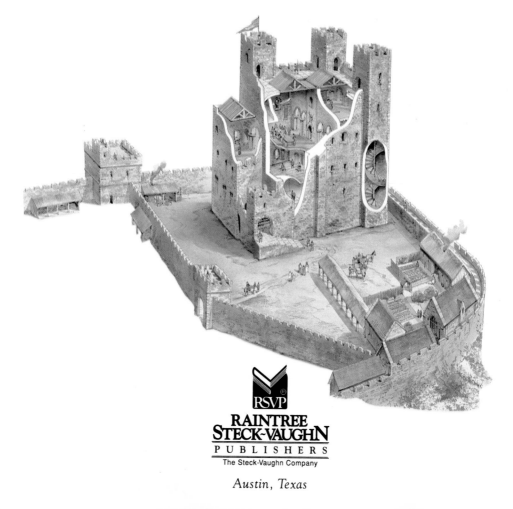

RSVP
RAINTREE
STECK-VAUGHN
PUBLISHERS
The Steck-Vaughn Company

Austin, Texas

Editor: Frank Tarsitano
Project Manager: Julie Klaus

Library of Congress Cataloging-in-Publication Data
Moss, Miriam.
        Forts and castles / written by Miriam Moss; illustrated by Chris Forsey.
            p.   cm — (Pointers)
        Includes index.
        Summary: Brief text and labeled illustrations discuss the history and
    architecture of several forts and castles, focusing on the protection they.
    afforded and mechanisms used in siege against them.
        ISBN 0-8114-6157-2 (hardcover binding)
        ISBN 0-8114-6339-7 (softcover binding)
        1. Fortification—Juvenile literature.   2. Castles—Juvenile literature.
    [1. Fortification   2. Castles.]   I. Forsey, Christopher, Ill.   II. Title.
    III. Series.
    UG401.M86   1994   93-11167
    355.7—dc20   CIP
                                                        AC

Printed and bound in the United States

    3 4 5 6 7 8 9 0 VH 99 98 97 96 95 94

6 The famous Lion Gate marks the entrance to the citadel. This approach to the gate runs between two guarded walls. This meant that an enemy would come under attack before reaching the gate.

Mycenae is the most famous Bronze Age citadel (fortress) in Greece. Built on a rocky hilltop, it lies half hidden by deep ravines and a protective wall. According to legend, Mycenae was the citadel of King Agamemnon. His legendary court was famous for its fabulous wealth.

In the 19th century, archaeologists began to excavate (dig up) the royal tombs at Mycenae. They found a hoard of golden treasures, including vases, face masks, and swords with golden hilts (handles).

Terrace

Temples

Grave circle

Bastion

Granary

Iron Age Hill Fort

Cadbury Castle was an Iron Age hill fort in Somerset, England. It was attacked by the Romans in about A.D. 60, and its Celtic inhabitants were massacred. By A.D. 500, however, Cadbury had become one of the largest, strongest forts in England.

Legend says that Cadbury Castle was the site of Camelot — the court of King Arthur and the famous Knights of the Round Table. The last time Cadbury was occupied was by the Saxon king, Ethelred II, from A.D. 1009-1016. He defended it against attack by the Danes.

▼ *A steep hill became harder for an enemy to climb if banks and ditches were dug around the sides. An embankment was built, then a ditch, and then a steep slope, all of which the attackers would have to cross to reach the castle. All this time, the defenders could use their weapons on the attackers.*

4 After the Roman massacre, the dead Celtic defenders were left unburied. Their bodies were probably torn apart by wolves. Ornaments have been found inside the gate, as well as over 100 iron weapons and scattered bones.

3 The hill had four or five lines of Iron Age embankments and ditches that attackers found very difficult to get past.

2 The main entrance passage to the fort was lined with stone and had a single guardroom above. Feet, hooves, and wheels have worn the rock path into a rut over 6 feet (1.8 m) deep.

1 During King Arthur's time, the defensive wall around the fort was made of a timber framework with plants or wickerwork on top. Earth and rubble were piled up, and the wall was finished off with a facing of stonework.

Rampart

5 The large feasting hall had a thatched roof and timber walls. The walls were coated with clay, pitch, or mud. Part of the hall was divided off as a private chamber.

5

6

Southwest gate tower

4

2

6 This is one of three, probably military, rectangular buildings which have been excavated at Cadbury.

1

Herod's Fortress

Masada stands on a mountaintop high above the desert near the Dead Sea in Israel. It was expanded by Herod the Great. In A.D. 73, a group of Jews used Masada as their base while they battled to gain freedom from Roman rule.

One night, the leader of the Jews persuaded his people to end their own lives rather than be taken prisoner. Each man had to kill his own family, and 10 men were chosen by lottery to kill the rest. The last remaining man had to set fire to the palace and then kill himself. When the Romans reached Masada, they were met with a terrible silence.

2 The wall surrounding the fortress had many towers as an additional defense. Inside the wall were 100 rooms.

1 The Roman King of Judea, Herod the Great, built a palace at Masada on three levels, overlooking the Dead Sea.

Snake-path gate

Storehouses

Bathhouse

Administrative building

Synagogue

3 The huge underground water cisterns were filled with rainwater. Two Jewish women and five children hid in the cisterns to escape from the Romans. They were the only survivors.

4 King Herod's western palace had a throne room which was decorated with a beautiful, multicolored mosaic. Part of this mosaic can still be seen today.

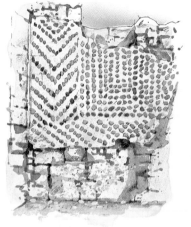

6 The bathhouse had a main pool and two small pools. One small pool collected water for the main pool. The other small pool was used by bathers to wash their hands and feet before entering the main pool.

5 Two parchment scrolls from the Bible were found buried under the synagogue floor. They may have been hidden there by the Jews before they died.

▲ *The church wall was decorated with unusual designs made from small stones and pieces of pottery.*

► Norman Keep

The castle in Rochester, England, is a good example of a Norman square keep. During the 11th and 12th centuries, the Normans (who came from France) occupied England and built many castles as strongholds. The castle served not only as a fortress but also as a home for its lord, a court, and a prison.

Rochester was one of the first English castles to be fortified with stone in place of timber. In 1215 it was defended against King John for seven weeks, despite being battered by stone-throwing machines. The fat of 40 pigs was used to set fire to the keep.

3 The tower was built after a siege in 1215. Its sturdily built wall was designed to deflect arrows, spears, and rocks away from the castle walls.

2 This part of the building protected the keep's entrance. Visitors had to pass through a small lobby, a guard tower, and a portcullis.

Mural tower

1 The outer bailey, or space between the walls, was used for sports contests. It also housed all the people who worked in the castle.

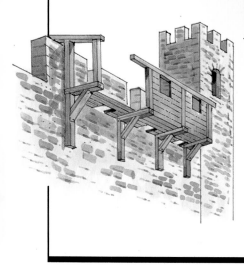

◄ The hoarding was a wooden gallery, which was attached to the top of the outer wall of the castle when it was under attack. The hoarding was held up by timber beams. It was used as a platform from which the defenders could drop heavy objects on the attackers below.

Battlements

4 The wall walk provided an excellent lookout point. After a siege in 1088, the old wooden defenses were replaced by stronger curtain walls of stone.

5 The mural gallery was used by the minstrels (musicians), as an exercise space during bad weather, or as an extra sleeping area.

Spiral staircase

6 The castle's keep was not only a military stronghold but also living quarters for its owners. Rochester keep had a basement and three floors above it.

Guard tower

Portcullis

Outer staircase

Inner bailey

Cross wall

Crusader Castle

Krak des Chevaliers, in Syria, was built in the 12th century by the Crusaders. They were fighting the Muslims for control of Jerusalem and the Holy Land. The castle was important because it controlled a mountain pass protecting the northern border of present-day Lebanon.

The castle's gigantic towers were made of massive stone blocks. There was a strong keep, the walls 27 feet (8.5 m) thick in places. The Great Hall was used for meetings of the Chapter of the Hospitaleers – the Crusader knights who governed Krak. The castle also contained a storeroom which could hold enough food to feed the garrison for five years.

1 The entrance to the castle included a long passage with guardrooms on either side opening onto a hidden moat between the inner and outer walls.

2 The Hall of Massive Pillars is on the side of the courtyard. It contained kitchens, dining rooms, and storerooms.

Windmill

Courtyard

Lookout tower

Machicolated galleries

3 A square tower jutted out from the outer walkway. It defended the narrow bridge of the aqueduct which supplied the moat with water.

4 The large hall that is protected by this wall contained a well and four bread ovens. It was also used as a warehouse. Toilets were built into the north wall.

5 The Great Hall was 88 feet (27 m) long and 24.6 feet (7.5 m) wide. It had a pointed roof.

6 A Crusader chapel was later converted into a mosque when the Muslims captured the fortress.

Aqueduct

The long arched entrance passage to the castle was built with a hairpin bend. It had gateways set in walls over 16 feet (5 m) thick with guardrooms on either side. A portcullis protected the entrance.

Medieval Castle

Conwy Castle, in North Wales, was built by Edward I. It was one of several new castles built to help him conquer Wales. Edward I was a well-traveled, experienced soldier. He knew that the corners on the old square keeps were blind spots, which meant they could easily be undermined by the enemy. So he built Conwy in a narrow rectangular shape defended by eight strong round towers.

Conwy was designed in two parts, one for the king, arranged like a castle within a castle which could be separately defended, and the other for the garrison overlooking the town. The building materials often had to be carried long distances, yet it took just four years to complete Conwy Castle, from 1283 to 1287. In those days the walls were whitewashed so that the castle stood out as a shining symbol of royal power.

Chapel tower

Stockhouse tower

Kitchen tower

Drawbridge

2 This wall extended from the castle to protect the town below and was built at the same time as the castle. The townspeople were protected not only by the wall but also by the castle and its defenses.

3 The king's tower was one of eight huge towers around the castle wall. These towers were used for defense and also for living quarters.

1 Loopholes were slitlike or cross-shaped openings in the castle wall. Archers could fire their arrows through them, safe from attack.

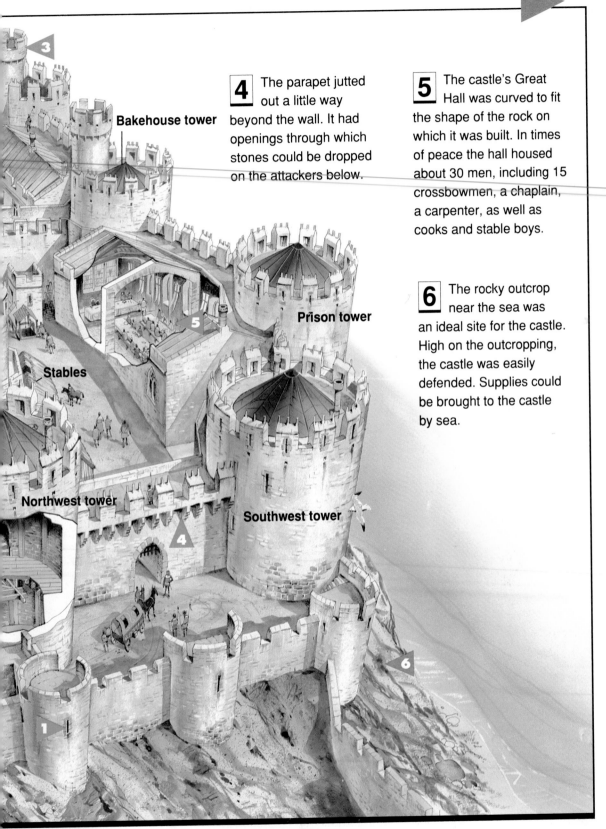

Bakehouse tower

4 The parapet jutted out a little way beyond the wall. It had openings through which stones could be dropped on the attackers below.

5 The castle's Great Hall was curved to fit the shape of the rock on which it was built. In times of peace the hall housed about 30 men, including 15 crossbowmen, a chaplain, a carpenter, as well as cooks and stable boys.

6 The rocky outcrop near the sea was an ideal site for the castle. High on the outcropping, the castle was easily defended. Supplies could be brought to the castle by sea.

Prison tower

Stables

Northwest tower

Southwest tower

14th-Century Castle

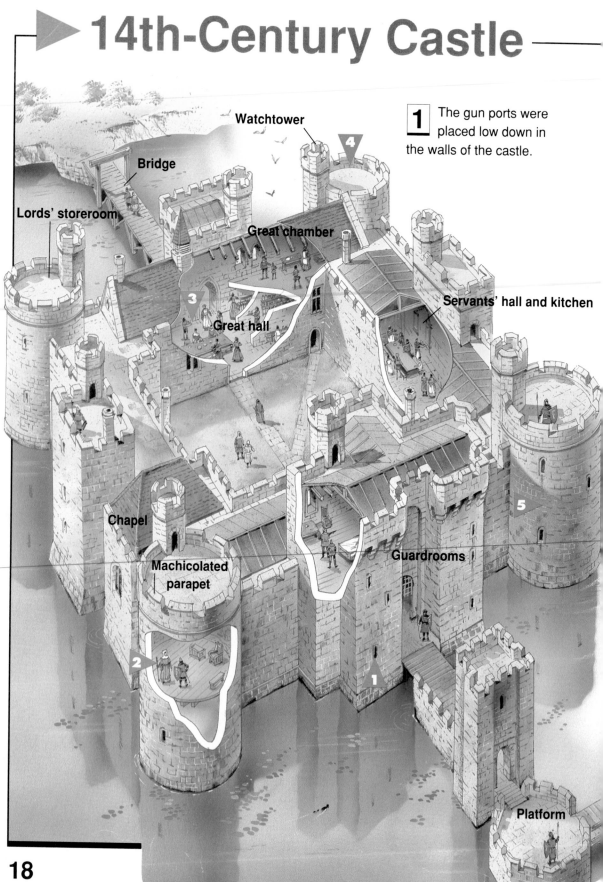

Watchtower

Bridge

1 The gun ports were placed low down in the walls of the castle.

Lords' storeroom

Great chamber

Servants' hall and kitchen

Great hall

Chapel

Machicolated parapet

Guardrooms

Platform

18

2 There were plenty of rooms for guests in the little chambers in the gatehouses and turrets.

3 Sir Edward's grand private rooms were away from the servants' quarters. He lived in style with different rooms for formal or family occasions.

4 The castle had a pigeon loft with 300 nests. The pigeons provided meat and feathers for mattresses and cushions.

5 The living quarters were protected by a moat with huge, round towers. The gatehouse and rear entrance tower guarded access to the castle.

Bodiam Castle was one of the last castles to be built in England. It was the result of centuries of experience in castle design and a good example of a castle which was built for defense but which was also a comfortable home.

In the 14th century, the French attacked several ports along the south coast of England. As a result, coastal defenses had to be made stronger. In 1386, a rich knight, Sir Edward Dalyngrigge, was given a royal license to fortify his manor house at Bodiam in Sussex. It became Bodiam Castle. Firearms were now being used for defense, and Bodiam was one of the first castles to have gun ports.

6 The wide moat was crossed by a bridge at right angles to the main approach. The postern (rear) gate also had defenses. These were similar to those at the front.

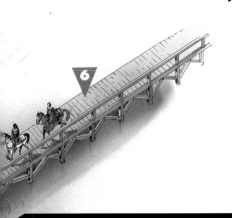

▶ The gatehouse had keyhole gun ports. The primitive guns were shaped like tubes and could be poked through the round hole. The gunner could look through the slit to take aim. Invaders coming over the bridge could be fired on from the castle.

French Château

In the 16th century, Francis I, the king of France, decided to build a splendid new castle, or château, on the banks of the Loire River at Chambord. A hunting lodge had originally stood on the same site. The château of Chambord was designed by the Italian architect, Domenico da Cortona. It was a huge project.

Some 1,800 men worked under three master

3 Chambord had an elaborate skyline of towers and turrets. They were a mixture of French and Italian architectural styles.

2 The château had 400 rooms which included private chambers for the king and his family, guest rooms, audience chambers, dining rooms, and kitchens.

1 In the center of the castle there was a huge spiral staircase. Two ramps twisted and turned, one above the other, and two people could climb up the stairs and not meet.

masons. These three men are thought to have changed the architect's original plans. They created the extraordinary mixture of plain and decorative styles found at Chambord. The château was designed along the lines of a fortified castle. The massive keep, corner towers, moat, and cannon openings in the battlements are all features more usually found in a castle.

4 The château was begun in 1519. It took many years to complete. The final details, including, the gilded lead roof of the keep, were completed in 1546.

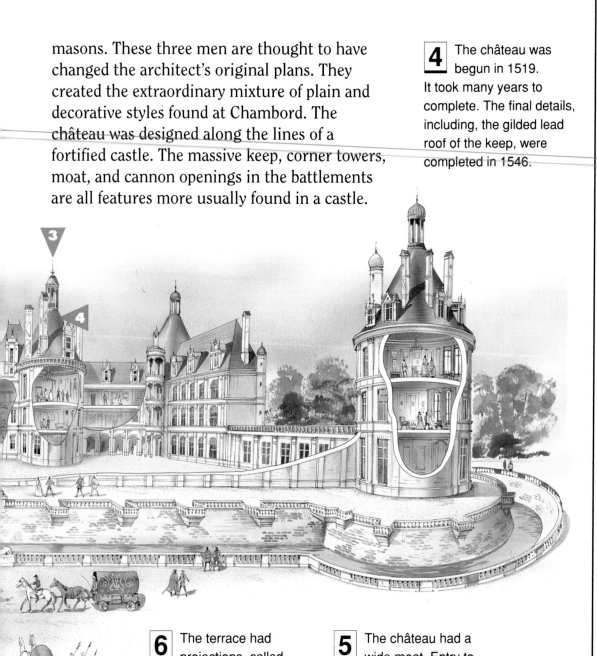

6 The terrace had projections, called corbels, within the walls. These were designed to hold cannons, although they were never used for this purpose.

5 The château had a wide moat. Entry to the château was across the moat by a bridge facing the keep.

Japanese Castle

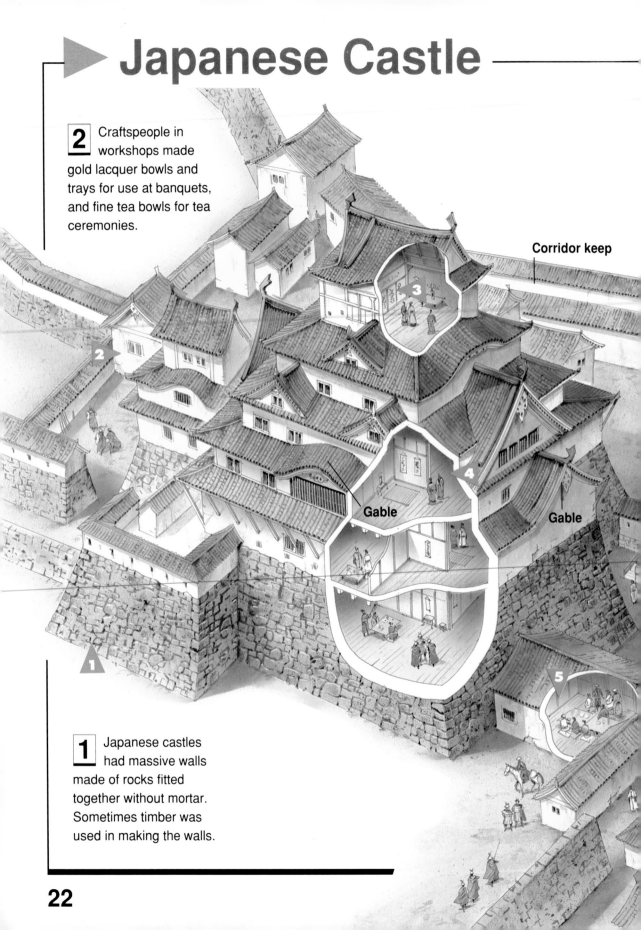

2 Craftspeople in workshops made gold lacquer bowls and trays for use at banquets, and fine tea bowls for tea ceremonies.

Corridor keep

Gable

Gable

1 Japanese castles had massive walls made of rocks fitted together without mortar. Sometimes timber was used in making the walls.

3 The walls, ceilings, and screens inside the castle were painted with beautiful scenes from nature. The painters used bright colors and gold leaf.

Most castles were built in Japan from 1568 to 1600 by powerful military warlords. The grand architecture and rich interiors of these castles were signs of the status and authority of the warlords. They constantly battled each other.

The finest surviving castle of this period is Himeji-jo (*jo* means castle in Japanese). The original building dated from the 14th century. It was enlarged by Hideyoshi, a military leader and master of siege warfare, who took possession of it in 1577. Himeji was given its present, majestic appearance in about 1600 by Ikeda Terumasa, another important military leader.

4 The castle's central area contained the donjon (keep). Japanese castles were unusual in having decorated gables (sloping ends of a pitched roof). Three smaller donjons were clustered around the main building.

5 The living quarters for the soldiers and servants of the powerful lord were in the castle. The castle was the center of trade, finance, learning, and the arts.

6 Loopholes in the wall were used for defense. Arrows or muskets were fired through the holes at the enemy.

Indian Fortress

4 The Divan-e Khass (Hall of Private Audience) was the most luxurious building. At each end of the hall, there was a saying written in gold: "!f on earth there is a paradise, then this is it, yes this is it, this is it."

In 1628 Shah Jahan became emperor of India. He decided to rebuild the old Indian city of Delhi. In 1638, he began planning his new city. Inside the city, he built a great fortified citadel containing a royal palace called the Red Fort, which was named after the deep-red color of its 98-foot (30 m) high sandstone walls.

Rang Mahal Painted Palace

Gardens

3 The Divan-e 'Amm (Hall of Public Audience) is made of a series of arches. The red sandstone used for these buildings was covered by a fine white plaster which was polished to look like marble.

2 Rows of pillars and screens of marble, which looked like fine lace, protected the beautiful palace gardens. The Canal of Paradise supplied water for the garden's fountains, waterfalls, and pools.

1 Each morning, the emperor inspected newly captured elephants. The new elephants were scrubbed clean, painted black, and then covered with embroidered cloth and silver bells.

The emperor's architects were famous for their beautiful buildings. Inside the palace enclosure were decorated smaller buildings, marble palaces, courtyards, and galleries with carved archways, marble floors, and high, domed ceilings. Many were decorated with gold and silver, and precious stones.

Lahore gate

5 The famous Peacock Throne stood in the Divan-e Khass on a huge marble slab. A magnificent gold canopy on pillars sparkling with emeralds covered the throne.

Moti Masjid Pearl Mosque

6 Hundreds of people were employed inside the citadel, for example, bakers, torch makers, perfume makers, and goldsmiths.

Civil War Fort

In the 19th century, a dispute about slavery led to the Civil War. The southern states seceded from the Union, and the country became divided. The war to bring the southern states back into the Union was fought between 1861 and 1865.

In early 1861, Fort Sumter in South Carolina faced a problem. It was a federal fort in the middle of Confederate territory. The small garrison of 10 officers and 73 men was under the command of Major Robert Anderson. The governor of South Carolina ordered Major Anderson to surrender. He refused, and thousands of Confederate troops surrounded the fort. They shelled the fort and set it on fire. The Civil War had begun.

2 Only one life was lost at Fort Sumter after the final surrender. When Major Anderson fired his last salute, a charge of gunpowder exploded and killed a gunner.

Soldiers' barracks

Building material

Stair tower

1 Fort Sumter was a five-sided stronghold made from brick. It stood on an island in Charleston harbor, South Carolina.

3 The fort was designed to hold about 650 men. There were enough provisions for 135 guns, arranged on different levels of the fort. The middle level was never finished, and guns were placed only in the top and bottom levels.

4 In 1865, Confederate troops abandoned the fort. Major Anderson, now a Union army general, returned to Fort Sumter on the anniversary of his departure to raise the flag he had lowered four years before.

▼ *Major Robert Anderson's courage in defending the fort in April 1861 made him famous in American history.*

Soldiers' barracks

Officers' quarters

Lantern

Sand

6 The walls of the fort were 5 to 10 feet (1.5 to 3 m) thick and 40 feet (12 m) above the water.

5 The strategic position of the fort on an island at the mouth of the harbor meant it could defend a wide area of land and sea.

Romantic Castle

Castles gradually stopped being used for defense, but people continued to build them to show off their wealth and importance. Rich people also built castles for nostalgic or romantic reasons, as they still do today.

King Louis II ("Mad" King Ludwig) started building his romantic castle, Neuschwanstein, in 1869. It stands high up in the mountains of Bavaria in southern Germany. Louis became king when he was only 18 years old. He was shy and felt misunderstood by the world around him. He decided to shut himself away and surround himself with beautiful things. Instead of an architect, he hired a theater set designer to build Neuschwanstein.

▲ Neuschwanstein was the favorite castle of the lonely king. The king loved the music written by Richard Wagner. He was especially fond of the opera Lohengrin in which the swan plays an important part.

2 In the king's bedroom on June 12, 1886, Louis was declared insane. He died mysteriously the next day. He and his doctor had gone for a walk, and both were found dead in a lake.

1 Huge amounts of materials were needed to build the castle. They were pulled up the mountain by a steam-operated crane. In one year 470 tons of marble, 1,580 tons of sandstone, and 400,000 bricks were used.

Dressing room

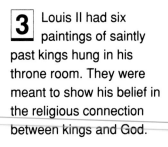

3 Louis II had six paintings of saintly past kings hung in his throne room. They were meant to show his belief in the religious connection between kings and God.

4 The name Neuschwanstein means "new swan stone." There was a swan in one form or another in almost every room in the castle. The swan was a symbol of purity and the king's favorite creature.

5 The king had a cave full of stalactites built between the living room and the study. These stalactites were made of plaster of paris.

6 The castle employed hundreds of people from the villages around it. For almost 20 years, they made their living from the building of the castle.

Singers' hall

Courtyard

Gatehouse

Glossary

Aqueduct
A bridge that carries water

Archaeologist
A person who studies the remains of past human life

Bailey
The outer court of a castle which could be defended from attack. There was sometimes an outer bailey and an inner bailey.

Bastion
A fortified stone wall

Battlements
A low structure built on a wall for defense or decoration

Bronze Age
The period of history which in ancient Greece lasted from about 2,000–1,000 B.C.

Chateau
A manor house, especially in France

Cistern
A tank for storing water, sometimes underground

Citadel
A stronghold inside or close to a city, or any strongly fortified building or refuge

Corbel
A stone or timber jutting out from a wall to support the end of a beam or a platform

Donjon
The medievel word for the keep of a castle

Fresco
A painting done in watercolors on wet plaster

Garrison
The place where troops are stationed to guard a fortified building

Gilded
Covered in gold or a substance looking like gold

Hording
A timber gallery built at the top of a wall or tower

Iron Age
The traditional name given to a time when smelting and use of iron was widespread. It followed the Bronze Age.

Keep
The main tower of a castle. People were often able to defend it without outside help.

Loophole
A slit- or cross-shaped opening in a castle wall, through which archers fired their arrows

Machicolation
An overhanging parapet or fighting gallery through which arrows, spears, and rocks could be dropped

Mason
A person skilled in working in and building with stone

Moat
A deep ditch around a castle, usually filled with water

Mosaic
A design or decoration made of small pieces of glass, pottery, or stone

Mosque
A Muslim place of worship

Nostalgic
When someone longs for the past

Parapet
A wall to protect a castle and its soldiers

Portcullis
A grating that slides up and down in grooves cut in the stones of a gate passage

Postern
A rear gate

Rampart
The embankment surrounding a fort, including any walls built for defense

Sally port
A hidden entrance from which defenders could mount a surprise attack on invaders

Scroll
A roll of parchment used for writing on

Siege
An operation carried out to capture a fortified place by surrounding it and not allowing people in or out

Synagogue
A building for Jewish religious services

Turret
A small tower

Undermine
To tunnel or dig under a building so it gradually gets weaker

► Index